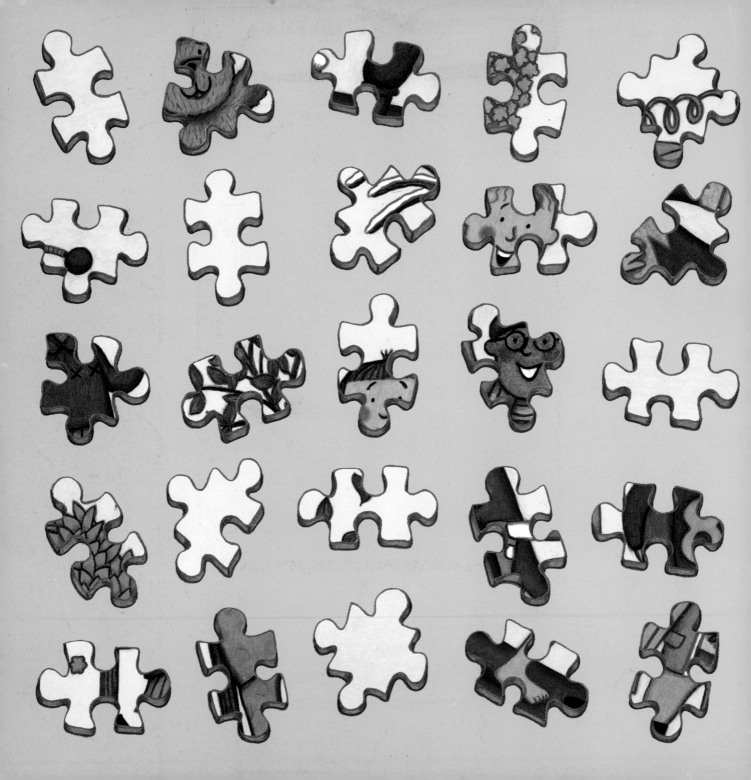

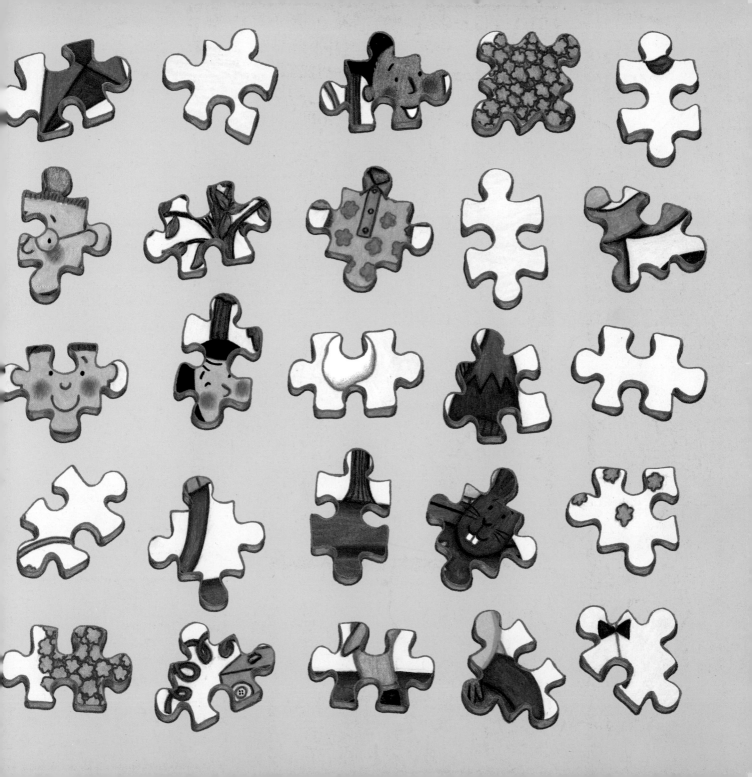

To Claire – NS

OXFORD
UNIVERSITY PRESS

Great Clarendon Street, Oxford OX2 6DP

Oxford University Press is a department of the University of Oxford.
It furthers the University's objective of excellence in research, scholarship,
and education by publishing worldwide in

Oxford New York

Athens Auckland Bangkok Bogotá Buenos Aires Calcutta
Cape Town Chennai Dar es Salaam Delhi Florence Hong Kong Istanbul
Karachi Kuala Lumpur Madrid Melbourne Mexico City Mumbai Nairobi
Paris São Paulo Singapore Taipei Tokyo Toronto Warsaw

with associated companies in Berlin Ibadan

Oxford is a registered trade mark of Oxford University Press
in the UK and in certain other countries

Arrangement and Selection copyright © Jill Bennett 1995
Illustrations copyright © Nick Sharratt 1995

The moral rights of the author and artist have been asserted

First published 1995
First published in paperback 1995
Reprinted in paperback 1995, 1996, 1997, 1998, 1999

British Library Cataloguing in Publication Data available

ISBN 0 19 276117 X

Printed in China

Acknowledgements

Marian Abbey, "My Bear", © 1995 Marian Abbey.
Stanley Cook, "Dens" from *The Poem Box*, © Stanley Cook
1992. First published by Blackie Childrens Books. Reprinted
with permission.
John Foster, "Going for a Swim", © John Foster 1995. Reprinted
by permission of the author.
Karla Kuskin, "Snow" from *Walker Read Aloud Rhymes*.
Published by Harper & Row Inc.
Michelle Magorian, "Sprinkles" from *Orange Paw Marks on the
Floor*. First published by Viking Books 1991. Reprinted with
permission.
Judith Nicholls, "Our Side of the Playground", © Judith
Nicholls 1995. Reprinted by permission of the author.
Jack Prelutsky, "Somersaults", "Colouring Books" from *Rainy
Day Saturday*. Published by Greenwillow Books 1980.
Michael Rosen, "I made a Robot" from *Who Drew on the Baby's
Head*. Reprinted by permission of Scholastic Publications Ltd.
Charles Thomson, "You Fell in the Puddle", © Charles
Thomson. Reprinted by permission of the author.
John Travers Moore, "Places" from *All Along the Way*, © 1973
Carolrhoda Books, reprinted by permission of the author.

Although every effort has been made to secure copyright
permission prior to publication, this has not proved possible in
some instances. If notified the publisher will be pleased to
rectify any errors or omissions at the earliest opportunity.

PLAYTIME POEMS

Collected by Jill Bennett
Illustrated by Nick Sharratt

Oxford University Press

Snow

We'll play in the snow
And stray in the snow
And stay in the snow
In a snow-white park.
We'll clown in the snow
And frown in the snow
Fall down in the snow
Till it's after dark.
We'll cook snow pies
In a big snow pan.
We'll make snow eyes
In a round snow man.
We'll sing snow songs
And chant snow chants
And roll in the snow
In our fat snow pants.
And when it's time to go home to eat
We'll have snow toes
On our frosted feet.

Karla Kuskin

I made a robot

I made a robot
out of boxes and cans
with buttons for its eyes
wooden spoons for its hands.

The robot's mouth was a McDonald's box
so it could open and shut.
One day I wasn't looking
and it clonked me on the nut.

Michael Rosen

Kite

A kite on the ground
is just paper and string
but up in the air
it will dance and sing.
A kite in the air
will dance and will caper
but back on the ground
is just string and paper.

Anon.

Somersaults

It's fun turning somersaults
and bouncing on the bed,
I walk on my hands
and I stand on my head.

I swing like a monkey
and I tumble and I shake,
I stretch and I bend,
but I never never break.

I wiggle like a worm
and I wriggle like an eel,
I hop like a rabbit
and I flop like a seal.

I leap like a frog
and I jump like a flea,
there must be rubber
inside of me.

Jack Prelutsky

You fell in the puddle

You fell in the puddle,
you fell off the swings,
you tripped on the dog
and bumped into things.

I know you're a Martian
in a space suit, but —
it would be a lot safer
without your eyes shut.

Charles Thomson

Going for a swim

On hot summer days, after school,
We go for a swim in the swimming pool.

As soon as I'm ready, I jump straight in.
I gasp as cold water splashes my skin.

I paddle across and cling to the side,
Then pull myself out to go on the slide.

I check that it's safe, then let myself go,
With a splash I crash into the water below.

I go underwater, but I don't care.
I come to the surface and breathe in some air.

Then I swim as fast as I can to the side
And I climb back up for another slide!

John Foster

Places

There are Go-through places
(Arches and doorways).
There are Crawl-under places
(Fence or wall).
But the Climb-up places
(Clear to the tiptops)
Are the very best places of all!

John Travers Moore

Sprinkled

Running away from the garden spray,
Dashing back as it spins,
Trying to beat it again as it whirls
And being the one who wins.

Dancing around on the cool wet ground,
Grass sticking up through my toes,
Being splashed hard when I'm not fast enough
From my feet to my knees to my nose.

Drips in my hair, but I don't care.
It's good getting wet in the sun.
Having a race with the sprinkler
And seeing how fast I can run.

Michelle Magorian

Our side of the playground . . .

Feet clump,
knees bump,
fists thump . . .

on our side of the playground!

School's out;
yell, shout,
gang's about . . .

on our side of the playground!

Temper flares,
scraps, dares.
Who cares . . .

on our side of the playground?

Run, chase,
We're ace!
Who'd face . . .

our side of the playground?

Whisper, stare,
shove, scare,
just BEWARE . . .

on OUR side of the playground!

Judith Nicholls

My bear

Bears have hairs
And furry faces.
Bears use stairs
As hiding places.

After breakfast,
Lunch and tea,
I play with my bear
And he plays with me.

Bears like streets
And parks and spaces.
Bears like treats
And tickling chases.

Bears are best
Because, you see,
I have my bear
And my bear has me.

Marian Abbey

My colouring book

When I fill in my colouring book,
how wonderful the pictures look!
I make things how I wish they were,
like leopards white and lavender,
and purple penguins, pea-green goats,
and elephants with orange coats,
yellow calves and rainbow roses,
black giraffes with silver noses,
forests thick with scarlet trees,
swarms of bright blue bumblebees,
zebras striped with grey and pink,
a golden crow, a lilac mink.
I colour all the rabbits red
and give a moose a turquoise head,
everything's my special way—
colouring's fun on a rainy day.

Jack Prelutsky

Dens

Dens are where the bears
Sleep the winter away
Or beasts that hunt by night
Lie hidden in the day
Or a den can be
A quilt or eiderdown
Spread from the settee
Over the back of a chair,
A dark and secret place
Where I have made my lair
And you can come to call on me —
If you dare.

Stanley Cook

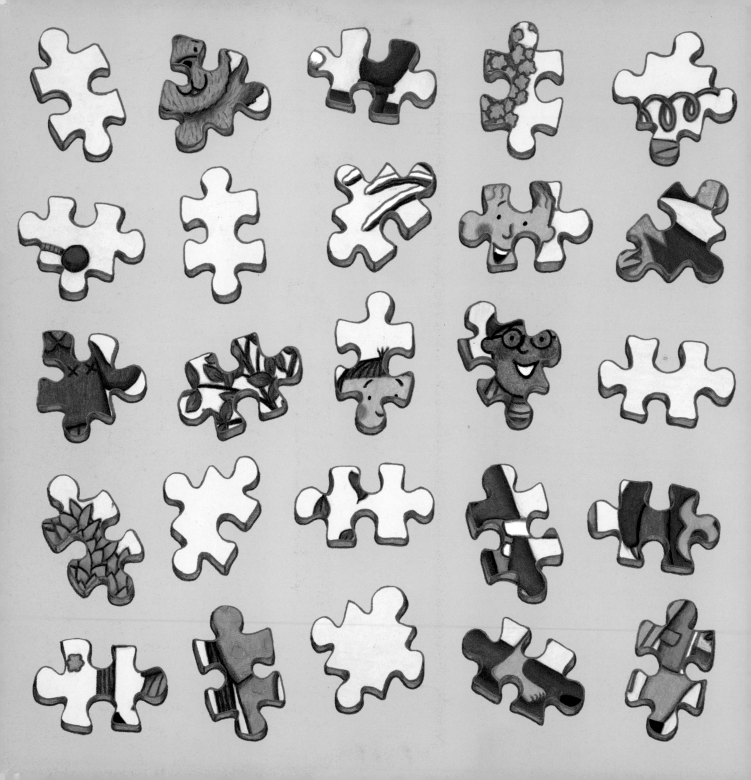

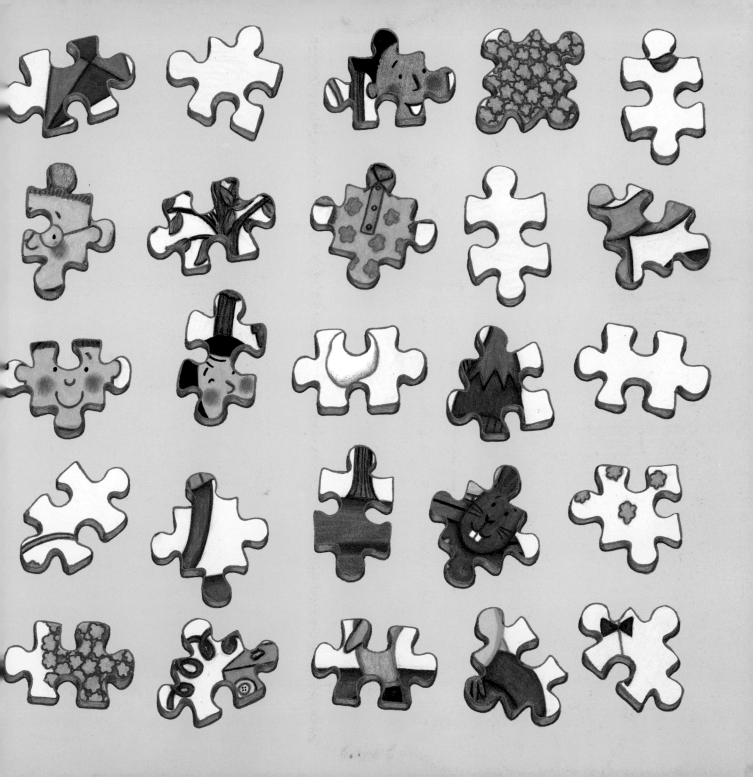